War of the Poems

by
Donley Dan Amick
and
Jeremy Paul Amick

PublishAmerica
Baltimore

© 2008 by Donley Dan Amick and Jeremy Paul Amick.
All rights reserved. No part of this book may be reproduced, stored in a retrieval system or transmitted in any form or by any means without the prior written permission of the publishers, except by a reviewer who may quote brief passages in a review to be printed in a newspaper, magazine or journal.

First printing

PublishAmerica has allowed this work to remain exactly as the author intended, verbatim, without editorial input.

ISBN: 1-60672-170-4
PUBLISHED BY PUBLISHAMERICA, LLLP
www.publishamerica.com
Baltimore

Printed in the United States of America

Jeremy would like to dedicate this book to friends, family, and acquaintances that have recently departed earth for more appealing stomping grounds: Abe Zey, Faye Clark, Jim Wilson & James Heil.
He would also like to dedicate this to his two sons, Chandler & Joey, who will surely carry on the Amick surname with both zeal and honor.

Dan would like to dedicate this book to the memory of his parents: Marion Paul and Opal Amick. Your two Marine Corps veteran sons miss you dearly.

Part I
Like Father...
by
Donley Dan Amick

Let Freedom Ring

They march past forty strong,
A platoon of Marines to fight Vietcong.
The fought and screamed and died that day,
They gave their life for the American way.

Sixteen died in a mortar attack
Of bravery there was no lack.
Fourteen or more were killed in a firefight
But not before they proved their might.

Three more went to a booby trap,
Now that place is remembered on a map.
Six were dead after their truck hit a mine,
They willingly put their life on the line.

Only one lived to return,
To that land where the flags they burn.
He was willing to stand up and fight,
Because he knew his country was right.

Why

Left home over a year ago,
To be sent where only God
And the Marine Corps know.
Ended up in South Vietnam,
Trying to bring peace and relative calm.

Came over with all the rest,
Spurred on by 40,000 of the country's best.
Yes; 40,000 dead and the wars not won,
But "the powers that be" say our jobs not done.

Maybe those vanished American's don't agree,
Because they came over to make this country free.
Many came and risked their life,
Maybe they saw a chance to end all strife.

Traveled 12,000 miles in defense of a cause,
Country at war 7 years without a pause.
Fighting this war with half our power,
Because of indecision in the "ivory tower."

It's with a sense of irony I leave,
Because I've witnessed a failure in what I believe.

War

Cheerfully I marched off to war
Didn't know about the unimaginable horror,
I went and joined—became a Marine
Member first-class of the war machine.

Never realized what I had done,
Now fighting a war that will never be won,
Oh, my poor Father and Mother,
Hope they stay my younger brother.

Now I am fighting in this far land,
But I am gladly lending a helping hand,
Am fighting this war that will never be won,
Hoping to save my unborn son.

Trained to kill like a man gone wild,
It makes no difference whether woman or child,
People back home never know the horrors we see,
Just as long as we fight to keep them free.

Yes, I am fighting for that pure white dove,
But I am not spreading Peace, Joy or Love,
Now my tour is over as a Marine,
I'm no longer a member of the war machine.

I'm ready to return to civilian life,
To settle down and take a wife,

Yet I'll never forget what I saw,
Because I have placed myself above God's law.

Even though I saw many people die,
For each one I still question "Why?"
From all of this one thing I did learn,
Freedom is not given, it's up to you to earn.

"Aspects of War"

When the War is through,
What's left for a Marine to do?
What I'm trained for is against my will,
All they taught me is how to kill.

10,000 men killed in a senseless war,
I know, I was there and saw the horror.
Death didn't care whether young or old,
They're all six feet under and chilly cold.

You earn a plastic body bag,
And for your casket, a bright new flag.
Now my two years are almost done,
But it'll be many years 'til the War is won.

Death

The past is a poor lover,
And the future is a distant dear.
I feel the Wings of Death hover near,
And walk thru the Valley of Shadow with fear.

Life remains very sweet,
But death is a demanding Master.
It's a crooked path that leads my wandering feet,
And ever I seem to go faster and faster

Now things are going very dark,
I think perhaps God has deserted me.
I know there'll be no rescuing Ark,
Because I can no longer see.

My body descends to Hell,
No pearly gates for me.
My soul I had to sell,
Upon my eyelids rest the entrance fee.

Untitled

The moon and the stars know of my love,
They heard me shout it to the heaven above.
Yes, I bared my soul in the night,
Let it be known with all my might.

It's hard to say what you want to tell,
Like being within a handmade hell.
Aching to release what's trapped within,
But fearing it would be a mortal sin.

Love can be many things,
Walking hand and hand with feet like wings.
Tripping through a spring dew morn,
Like the first two people ever born.

Love is knowing what's right all along,
But going ahead and doing wrong.
Standing ten feet tall in your own sight,
Hoping things turn out right.

Love is watching winter close down tight,
Shutting off the sun and light.
Lovely green plants turning brown,
Gently drooping their heads down.

Love is feeling mellow and pure,
Seeing the one you love and being sure.

Lying beneath a shady oak tree,
Talking in gentle tones and feeling free.

Yes, love s a new rebirth,
And a smile full of laughter and mirth.

War is Hell

War is Hell,
Gut shaking fear with no one to tell.
Your buddies all dead,
Killed by a small piece of lead.

Mortars in the dark,
You escape without a mark.
Crying out in dreadful need,
Watching your friends all bleed.

Screaming and yelling in the night,
Realizing it's for your life you fight.
Laying in a muddy foxhole,
To live longer you'd sell your soul.

Untitled

In the dead of night,
The dead are quiet.
The battle may be won,
But the war isn't done.

Fighting this war so unfair,
For a "Silent Majority" that doesn't care.
Every day more young men die,
Each one proves that politicians lie.

With piercing screams the dead protest,
Come in the dark and disturb my rest.
Rob me of sleep night by night,
Make it an effort to carry on in the light.

But what can you say,
Just try to live day by day.

Coming Home

22 more days to go,
Soon I'll be coming home you know.
After a long year in the Nam,
Finally achieving a sense of calm.

Don't know if I've done any good,
But I've tried all I could.
Sitting in the dark endless nights,
Aching for home and cheerful lights.

Time has passed very-slow,
Now it's almost time to go.
Find myself reluctant to pack,
Even though it is to go back.

After awhile the war gets in your blood,
You no longer care about dust or mud.
Have to force yourself to get ready to go,
Soon you'll be coming home you know.

Part II

...Like Son

by

Jeremy Paul

Our Path

If the road to hell is paved with good intentions
There'll surely be a freeway in my name
I've always meant well and tried to do right
But my follow-through ends crippled and lame

Modern America, there's not time for review
Move now, move forward and move fast
Make your money, maybe spend some before death
Spinning blindly through life; no time to look back

The drive to make better can in the end be our ruin
And the children are most often the victims
I don't have the time to raise you up proper
In a few years we can make our amends

No responsibility for our actions, the world is to blame
Why does everyone concentrate their attentions on me?
A creation of deceptions that we'll finally realize
When of our flesh, blood and breath we are relieved

Learning In Perpetuity

Inside the stone cold walls once again
It's very different this time
Now I have to pay for it
It's also at a higher mentality level
First Russellville High
Then U.S. Army Quartermaster
Now Columbia College
Will it someday reach an end?
Life's a never-ending learning process
What in the hell did I get myself into

Sigmund

Mr. Freud has taken the time to classify my dreams
Some are said to be very intelligible and keen
The rest we find incoherent; complicated and meaningless
Yet I seldom find myself satisfied with faux things I've seen

As the memory of the night flitters away on the winds of waking
Psychical activity has never been in question
As my brain runs a marathon of images through the night
Wishes and desires that are not realized in consciousness

Are accomplished with perfection after my sun sets
My subconscious tends to ignore my remonstrations of forgetfulness

Angst-fraught Hope

Was in a good mood
Then it became wasted
Shot in the head!
Now depressed thoughts resound
What to do?
Maybe it'll work itself out...in time
Yes.
For the better—
I hope.

Ours

Can totalitarianism exist
In a country whose foundation
Is based primarily on the belief
That family and freedom rule the roost?

Yes, it does exist-
I can see it all around us
From the rancid father telling the son
To get a haircut or find a new home
Or the government setting the drinking age
At an arbitrary twenty-one

It is our hair, our lungs, our livers
And our lives
We exist as sentient and intelligent beings
At the zenith of the food chain and consciousness
And if you can't learn to accept that
Then we have become little better
Than useless animals

Education

I am now here as the student
With explicit orders to learn
Required to acquire the credit
And hoping not to be spurned

I seek my knowledge in a separate style
The instructor just doesn't comprehend
How to prove this without any adverse effect?
A sense of direction I plead to be sent

Scornful of doubt, where is the end?
Modern education is a farce; too repetitious
Don't force me to bow; I've no will to conform
I refuse to ever feed from your filthy dish

Overtures of Anxiety

I have failed yet another relationship
That possessed a few shimmers of hope
A disgrace and sadness so often found
That I have now learned to embrace it
The weak claim that it's not my fault
Does not allay the pain I again exude
The loneliness of an empty house
Is the most disturbing sound I've discovered
The sordid thoughts that plow across my mind
Are laced with disruptive destruction
All eyes are upon you within your mind
Though none are in physical proximity
Escorting you to an approaching land of madness
A pool of sadness and self-blame
Perpetuates your descent into a shameful ire
The life of a divorced young male
Riddled with overtures of anxiety

Guns and Genetics

They have all but banished the Native American
To a government subsidized exile and life of poverty
Just meager tribesmen
Scratching a living from the harrowed earth
A forced immigration to the west
Which fathered an extended period
Of starvation topped with deceitful trades
And the sights of rifles aimed at their backs
Many fell ill only to helplessly witness
Their warriors and children
Wither into an emaciated state
Contradictory of their former glory
A sadness that cannot be denied
A disgrace that can't be rectified

Failed Relationships

I'm now 30 years old
And don't have time for
These petty teenage love games
I've sustained very severe
Emotional damage
Made irreparable by
Vindictive tendencies.
I've fought too many
Love battles;
On too many fronts
How much heartache
Can one endure?
Before complete and utter
Failure of all emotional systems?
This is why I've developed
A perpetual distrust
Of the motives of women.
I feel as though
I have played
An involuntary part
In some cruel, cruel plan…
Failed relationships have
Become my unquestionable
…specialty

House of Lords

The House of Lords in old Joplin
Once perched boldly on Main Street
The pinnacle of manly desires
Funded by riches exhumed from local mines
Several stories of sin and deceit
Designed to extirpate passions and fires
Gambling, women, sleep and food
The evils of humanity exudes from their flesh
Their wicked behaviors have left them blind
To the impending heavenly ire

Famine Ship

The *famine ship creeps into the misty harbor*
An *inexplicable sadness shrouds its arrival*
The *stiff corpse of a famished infant*
Cradled *in the arms of an emotionally-ruined mother*
A *child never to experience the soft promise of freedom*
Cholera *raced through the overcrowded ship*
As *quickly as a rumor in a small village*
Obliterating *both life and hope*
A *fading father bent over a filthy crate*
In *a hacking and mucous-filled stupor*
Gone *is the promise of a land filled with opportunity*
Pleasant *expectations replaced with death and decay*
Left *begging for life's table scraps*
A *people expected to remain satisfied...and silent*
In *a world of rotten potatoes and molded bread*
The *hard-working Irish forced from their homeland*
More *unfortunate victims of failed English colonialism*

Running From Change

You will never find paradise here on earth
Because it is a transient objective
Our age, insights and personal morals
Always remain in a constant state of flux
Too often we feel obligated to bolt from change
Knowing that it will become the inevitable
Refusing to embrace it until threatened or forced
Then looking back in utter astonishment
Wondering why we were ever worried
And questioning why it didn't' come around sooner
Or why we let our fear consume
What few moments of peace we were granted

Sinister History

Nazi occultism
Secret medieval rituals
Tucked away in a castle
Nestled in soft-rolling hills
Of northwest Germany
Concealing the malicious
And hardened Gestapo
Mr. Heinrich Himmler
Creating false links to the supermen of Atlantis...
And working the propaganda machine
Expanding the Germanic Empire
The quest for the Holy Grail
And pure Aryan blood
Will create millions of victims
...Otto Ran leads the way

Venting

Venting my demons in my own personal way
Numerous times it ends in a lay
Mother looks on in awkward dismay
Father has flashbacks of yesterday

I'm tired of being labeled as ruthless and lewd
Sometimes the say the epitome of rude
I've even heard mentioned the adjective "crude"
Remaining virtually aloof of my shifting moods

But sometimes I think that I'm just stuck in a rut
So I continue forward as I feel that I must
Then rewarded with a gift of passion and lust
In fear that my libido will begin to rust

Propagated by alcohol and a lack of inhibitions
With prayers I beg for someone to listen
And possibly understand my personal mission
To prevent me from reaching an eternal remission

Radio is a background specter-like dream; I sit here pondering my present love. Like so many before, I'm sure this is the one, perfect subject for a forlorn winter's day. This one can surely be different...I need to make this one work. No double talk, no blinding lies, no excess...yet sex is good. Long blonde tresses propagate the ostensibly self-destructive bulge in my jeans. I love my girl as the world is her. I must find money, a house and most importantly, privacy. Utter resentment for communal living creates difficulties and makes for a rabid coexistence. I like my barroom buddies and very occasional family visits, but I feel as though she has become my chalice of life. All I need to do now is learn how to traverse the tumultuous plains of modern living. Though not verdant and soothing as a spring mountain valley, our relationship will flourish...it must. I continually grow tired of the dejection and devilish female sneers.

Death Watch

Death Watch 22
The dreadful mark of an additional year
Clarification of pain and ignorance
Yet still unscathed
Continued regression
I feel alright...
Isn't that all that truly matters?

Lost Trust

The wan grin on the face of demise poised sarcastically in
the back of my mind
Reminding me of the overgrown paths that are now left
embarrassingly behind
We constantly migrate from one dream to another,
finally just giving up with age
Wondering where our youth disappeared,
staring into a future now blind and afraid

You keep searching for new things to lift your spirits;
but they eventually let you down
Our inner kingdoms crumbled before they are built,
robbing us all of our crowns
Then strange sympathies we seem to find from strangers
promising to lift us back up
But never again will we wholly trust those we're convinced
to be foul and corrupt

Impeccable ignorance
Double-standard leadership
The onus of honesty does not exist
Knee-high morals of the nineties
Will complete our hopes of destruction
Reprobates abounding
"The End" resounding
Financial entrapment
Screams "No Change!"
Rescind your dreams
Pray to the demons
To be gentle and merciful
In the jaunt to uncertain oblivion
Querulous souls
Pyrrhic loss

Oh dear Lord,
Thirty years under my belt
And a waistline growing quicker
Than my age
The grace of time I have not seen
A hairline that has moved
To the southern regions
Now a shiny and forsaken forehead
I convince myself it's just less to comb
But the greater society disagrees
But I don't need the beauty
A search I don't welcome
Ignominy I'll not be forced into

Will my life amount to anything-never to be famous?
Haven't truly learned freedom
And all my classmates doing quite well
It feels as though I'm suited to question reason
Too tied down unlike Kerouac and Morrison
What about Hemingway?
Children and wife
Yet so many others with rich parents
Everyone but me getting lucky breaks in life
So many have beautiful wives but try to make other girls
——————and then Big John always talking about dying

Contact Lenses

Contact lenses have changed my life
From the wretched constriction of glasses
I have a perfect spectrum of vision once more
Again part of the pretty masses

My nerdy days of spectacled imagery
Now just a visage of the past
I now feel like a very handsome man
Let's pray that my new-found hope does last

The miniscule lenses that I place on my eyes
Have brought my world back into view
Now that I've experienced this marvel of science
All spectacles I will eschew.

It Has All Been Done

Everything has been said before, whether it has been in poetry or novel, or even in the songs that we sing. An English teacher once told me that poetry is nothing more than the human condition retold. He believed that every generation must state it again for it to be recognized. There is some truth to that; nothing we read can really be completely original. The nuclear bomb, in essence, is not new; if you evaluate it, it is nothing more than an updated form of destruction. A modernized version of ancient warfare. So everyone, write! Let your generation have a modernized outlook on previously discovered views and insights.

Cheated

Vast verdant countryside decisively chopped and ravaged
To unroll new highways to be used by the masses
Flashing towers and lights to warn distant airplanes
Watch the white lines into town; so drunk and insane
Highways spattered with billboards and homes
The plains are gone and forgotten, no buffalo left to roam
Nicely wrapped and hidden in our biased history books
Who's been screwed the worst by these white-devil crooks

War Trauma

Blood basted shores, our soldiers scorned
Machine gun danger, our futile anger
Wounded sergeant, the blind are in charge
Sending them into this deadly den
Safe at the Pentagon while mothers worry
About their children's feet upon foreign soil
Praying that all is well
Post-Traumatic nightmares
That will never be quelled

Too Kind

The fresh-green grass speckled with clover and dandelion
The soothing fragrance of lilac transported by the breeze
The innocent chirp of an insignificant little finch
These peaceful moments are the ones I wish to seize

Few and far between is the calming effect of nature
Our hasty lives divert us from the serene

Mother Nature has carried away my youthful energy
The searing heat taking its toll on my gumption
Yet she is much too kind to her human children
Even in light of our insatiable resource consumption

Why Question?

Why fight? Why fuck?
Why be broken and down on your luck?
Forget depression—
But keep the drinking
Which has really gotten me
Abstractly thinking
Why must we work,
When we can play all day?
Do we really need structure,
To show us the way?
I don't know, I'm asking you
In my shoes what would you do?
The end isn't near
I think it's a farce
When speaking of this
Consider the source
I may be mistaken
I'm too often wrong
But it really doesn't matter
Since we're not here very long

Worthy Battle

Should I enjoy the pleasures of another woman?
While still imprisoned and duty bound-
Will I commit myself to the devil so,
Never again to be glory bound

Such baneful emotions I must fight
On the basis of the minute
Trying to discover relief in the strangest ways
To see these tortures diminish

Due to suffer
The unique pangs
Of this seemingly
Endless torture
I am young
But feel as though I have fallen
No longer high-speed
Seeping slowly from my veins

Welcome Sacrifice

Writing in a most drunken stupor
A dozen thoughts scribbled across my mind
Bequeathing freely to posterity
The thoughts I believe to be most divine

I'm caught up in a maelstrom of discord
Something that doesn't seem stoppable
Reeling dizzyingly with a madness
My thoughts have turned despicable

Return me to God, my family and love
I'm not what I once grew to love
An unrecognizable madman I have become
I need the help launched from above

There's always hope; possibly a new future
A gamble I'm ready and willing to take
For my family and personal sanity
Any sacrifice I am willing to make

Lonely Trip

The patio in my yard provides me eyes to the world
As it can exist on a handful of acres
People passing by in a shelled existence
Petty minds full of hope or rancor

Are they pondering Jesus or which beer to purchase?
Does anyone actually feel alike?
We all suffer the pains of our common existence
Crossing paths throughout life's erratic hike

I'll just keep traveling down my lonely highway
Even though the lights of direction have disappeared
I certain that I'm now on my own
And it's up to me to find the true way

Another Fine Mess

Double ties
Twisted lies
Which one is the best for me?

One has a child
One seems too wild
I feel blind, but I'll learn to see

Caught again in a twisted mess
Have to decide which one is the best
If I am to ever be set free

I'll find my way out
My success I'll then tout
Yet return to the same agony

Put out or get out!
How often have you heard that phrase?
The yearning to keep searching,
For the ideal and satisfying lay.

In my youth I was a pig,
The best of the worst.
Until one woman finally came along,
And quenched my unfulfilled thirst.

This one appears to have it all,
Beautiful, with a mind to match,
Now I can only hope,
That she's been built to last.

Imminent Domain

Ready or not, here it comes
The politicians got their act together
And funds are finally appropriated
The destruction of homes that have been here for decades
Everyone says that it is an utter shame and loss
But they quickly forget this under the convenience of quicker highways
The plague of perpetually modified plans
...Imminent domain
Bulldozers dig with much alacrity
Highway 50 is unrolling new paths towards Centertown
Leaving a path of progress and destruction in its wake
Consuming homes, farms, forests and memories
Eviscerating the family-owned landscape
Eradicating childhood flashbacks and recollections

Redneck Musings

I only got as far as the sawmill when the old truck quit
"I'll give you fifty bucks for that old rag."
"Sure thing, but I'm keeping the battery."
That old truck has left me walking too many times
I heard that ol' junk motor knockin'
And found a hole in the block as big as a beer can
She had the power though, in her day
I'd tie a rope to a stump, just ease out the clutch
And rip that hunk of wood right out of the ground

Awaited Egocentrism

In my little microcosm of nothing
I've become a celebrity
"They recognize my face from the paper!"
I scream joyfully to myself
There are those who malign me
But I refuse to hear their voices

Twisted Justification

Off to earn a buck
So that I can practice my freedom
Of giving it away
Neither poor nor rich
Not a governmental child
Have to look out for myself and my interests
Equal opportunity?
I'm not sure it exists
Everyone carries prejudice—
Some are just better at justifying theirs

Our Home

The setting sun really blesses my eyes
I hear the children and their cheerful cries
Warm Missouri evenings are the best I've ever known
Watching the rising plants in the little garden I've sown
The place we are raised will always be the best
It is here I was born and will probably be laid to rest
No one can truly understand; looking in from the outside
We may appear quite common but know how to survive
Common sense is our guide, not silly fashions or political whims
Here we have nothing to hide but everything to defend

Salvation Paid

I sense the eyes focused on the back of my skull
Viewing intently with masked judgment
"What's he doing here?" they internally question
Did he finally find time for the sacraments?

Forget not that our forgiveness was purchased for a price
The most expensive blood this world has ever known
A price that no amount of currency can realize
A garden of life that has been unselfishly sown

Organized religion has become much too convenient
Structured services meant not to offend anyone
Fading are the sermons of hellfire and brimstone
Creating a new paradigm where anything goes
New beliefs as lonely and depressing as a wooden cross
Poignantly placed beside an interstate

I Do

What are your thoughts on me?
Are they dour-soaked and malicious,
Or bustling with amorous energies?
I couldn't handle being only a fad

A catharsis of hope
How I'd surely be happy with you
Premonition of your pursed lips
Poised in a meaningfully deserved "I do!"

Have You?

Have you ever sat
Alone
Separated from
Your daily realities
Staring into
Nowhere and nothing
Free from any thoughts
Clanking through your
Guilt-ridden mind
Focused on
Nothing,
No complex
Worries or concerns
In a dimension lacking
Awareness of the concept of time

Flaunted Sin

She slips into my life very quietly
And when I see her
The fire inside me burns
I wish that I could make
Her notice me very soon
I can feel my passions begin to churn

Everything about her is beautiful
Her lips, her hair, her skin
For her I would definitely sin
Even though she always gets looks
From many different men
Flaunting a body that's built
To make the holiest of men commit sin

Alaska

Alaska.
One of the few states I long to go,
Rolling landscapes smothered in snow
With its beautiful snowcapped mountains,
And numerous geysers that shoot up like fountains
Behold the beautiful forests teeming with wildlife
The coastline dotted with seagulls and their cries
Someday I will make it and eventually see
The place I have always longed to be

Censorship

They say we're going to hell
They claim that we we'll eventually burn
All I can say is "Oh well."
I've grown accustomed to being spurned

I'm sick and tired of the censorship
Government controlling whatever we see
Stray from the rules that they have set
And the FCC will assign you a fee

We do not exist in a communist regime
We have been given minds of our own
To me it truly appears to be
That this whole thing has been overblown

You Feds have been to busy taking bribes
To foist on us laws by which to abide

Shimmering amalgamation of gases floating millions of miles away
Lends a peace and comfort to the disturbed mind
A simple reminder of an insignificant existence
At this petty level the argument of fate vs. choice is of no consequence
Wow, the moon sure is bright tonight.

Macbeth

Oh, the yearning to be king
And the willingness to murder
Is it ever truly worth it?
The three witches will bring
A reckless madness to your mind
Crazy thoughts that everyone can read
False blame that will never take root
What goes around comes around
...Someday
An ignominious defeat is inevitable
Malcolm will not stand by unjustly scorned

Printed in the United States
128589LV00010B/1/P